THE CYCLING
HANDBOOK

THE CYCLING HANDBOOK

First published by Parragon in 2013

Parragon
Chartist House
15–17 Trim Street
Bath BA1 1HA, UK
www.parragon.com

Copyright © Parragon Books Ltd 2013

Written by Ruth Jarvis
Illustrated by Harriet Seed
Cover and internal design by Michael Duffy

ISBN 978-1-4723-3028-4

Printed in China

Bath • New York • Singapore • Hong Kong • Cologne • Delhi
Melbourne • Amsterdam • Johannesburg • Shenzhen

contents

Why bike is best

If you're looking at this book, congratulations. You're about to discover a whole world of two-wheeled pleasure that really could change your life. Remember the rush of wonder you felt as a kid the moment you realized you were piloting your bike all by yourself? Get in the saddle as an adult and you'll experience just the same sense of joy and independence.

Bicycles are a little marvel of physics. They turn human strength into a miracle of forward motion far more efficient than our funny two-legged gait. In the time it would take an elite athlete to run a 26-mile marathon, an elite cyclist would be zipping towards the finish line for the third time. Even a distinctly non-elite, everyday rider would be hard pressed to ride at less than ten miles an hour. At bike-speed, out in the fresh air, you become immersed in your surroundings, and a ride becomes a new way of experiencing the world. All this, and the fuel you need isn't planet-damaging, pocket-damaging oil, just normal healthy human food (and perhaps even cake on special occasions).

Riding even short distances every day can help you stay at a healthy weight, and pedalling fast is one of the best ways to improve cardio fitness - but cycling can also be a very gentle form of exercise and requires no special skills, so it's suitable for everyone. If you find it hard to carve out time to keep fit, cycling is the answer - just make a regular journey by bike instead of car or public transport and it may even save you time. You'll also be helping keep down traffic congestion, which is often caused by lots of cars making short, bikeable journeys.

When you take up riding a bike, it feels like you've joined a worldwide club of riders who've all discovered the best-ever transport secret. You'll find yourself having breakfast at cycle cafés, chatting at parties about great local routes, holidaying on two wheels and lending your settee to cycle tourists from the other side of the world. But cycling is a very broad church and you can choose which pew you want to sit in. Whether you want to make everyday journeys, occasional short pleasure rides or embrace cycling as a sport or lifestyle, you'll find all the information you need to get started safely in this handbook - and you can keep a record of your progress in the accompanying journal. Because once you've discovered (or rediscovered) the pleasures of cycling, you'll never look back.

Happy pedalling!

What kind of rider are you?

No two cyclists are the same. Everyone has their own needs, preferences, comfort zone and personal style. Depending on these, you are likely to fall somewhere within a category of riders. Just like any activity or social scene, cycling has its own 'tribes'.

amsterdammer

The Netherlands has become a role model for any country wishing to be properly cycle friendly. Cycling in Amsterdam is as normal as getting in the car in Los Angeles. No-one makes a big song and dance about it, and the design and rules of the road usually put the bike first. Amsterdammers aren't even that fussed about getting anywhere very fast, but then they don't have to waste time fiddling with special clothing or accessories, which they tend to disdain. Bicycles are designed for comfort and practicality, with features like built-in locks and dynamo lights allowing you to rock up, sit down and take off with no fuss.

This model of cycling appeals to people in towns where distances aren't too great, hills aren't too steep and the road design is relatively safe. Women, particularly, like to be able to wear their normal wardrobe while cycling. If you love the convenience of cycling but don't buy into all the cultural and sporting folderol that surrounds it, then you're an Amsterdammer.

urban roadster

For roadster, read hipster on a bike. Like the Amsterdammer, urban roadsters are happy to wear the same outfit for riding and relaxation, but in their case it's gently slanted towards the bike, with one eye on understated chic and the other on retro cycling culture. A peaked race cap, well-cut shirt, street trousers or long shorts designed to be comfortable in the saddle and hand-made leather shoes, all in distinctly non-fluoro colours, are the apogee of the style, for both guys and girls.

Most urban roadsters ride pretty much everywhere, but the odds are that they take their bike indoors at their destination, because it's likely to be a handsome single-speed or fixed-wheel that might as well have 'steal me!' written on its frame. Actually, the frame will probably bear only the name of the maker: to add a lock or rack would spoil its lines, so riders carry these in messenger bags.

Roadsters cherish their mounts, and hang around cycle cafés and internet forums discussing the latest type of seat post with their bikie mates. You'll find them in the trendier quarters of cities such as London and Los Angeles.

TIP

Urban roadsters don't like to disfigure their bike with boring old mudguards. But neither do they want a 'skunk stripe' of road rain splashing up their back. So when the heavens open, they find an old plastic bottle and wedge it between the seat stays just above the back wheel. Copy their style, especially if you live in a (usually) sunny climate.

career commuter

Let's face it, commuting by car or public transport can be expensive. Plus it subjects you to delays that your boss might not like. Career commuters may or may not enjoy cycling for fun at other times, but they've made a commitment to riding to work every day, come rain or shine, and their choice of bike and gear reflects that. Their mount will be a reliable workhorse, often a hybrid or town bike with an upright position and gears that make for an efficient ride whatever the gradient, and they will be equipped to ride in the rain and dark, with waterproof jacket and trousers, decent lights and mudguards. They may carry a backpack or a briefcase that clips to a rack. If they arrive in town by train, they may bring a folding bike or use a public bike rental scheme.

If you are thinking of commuting by bike, find out whether your workplace offers a ride-to-work programme. Benefits may include financial help with buying a bike and facilities such as cycle parking and a shower.

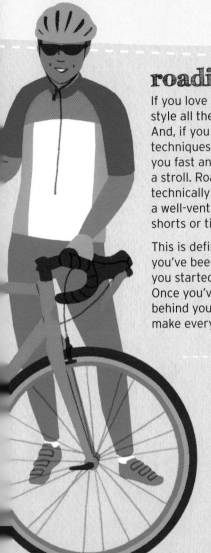

roadie

If you love road riding, you may find it your preferred cycling style all the time, not only on weekend rides but around town. And, if you have the skills and the fitness, why not? The techniques you'll learn on sportives and training rides will make you fast and nimble in traffic and 20-mile journeys will seem like a stroll. Road riders equip themselves with a lightweight, technically slick road bike and dress in equally technical gear: a well-ventilated helmet, eye protection, a team jersey, cycle shorts or tights and shoes that clip in to the pedals.

This is definitely a style to be earned, not learned. Either you've been doing this since you were a lanky teenager, or you started off as an around-town rider and then got the bug. Once you've joined a cycle club and started putting the miles behind you, you'll find you want to upgrade your bike and make every ride a training ride.

character cyclist

Cyclists have always been known as great eccentrics, and there's plenty of scope for following your own style. Currently, there's a vogue for harking back to the clothing (if not the steeds) of the early days of cycling, complete with facial hair, tweeds, capes and plus-fours. Or bloomers, for girls. But feel free to follow a style that's all your own, from a dress suit to - on the day of the Naked Bike Ride (see page 59) - your birthday suit.

Choosing your wheels

A bike's a bike, right? A couple of wheels, some pedals and a brake or two and you'll be riding off into the sunset. Well, yes and no. You'll hear a lot – often from bike manufacturers – about how a particular kind of cycle is absolutely essential for a particular kind of riding, preferably a brand, shiny new one, with lots of bells and whistles. (Well, bells, at least; you'll have to bring your own whistle.)

In fact, pretty much any steed will get you happily from A to B, as long as it's comfortable and in good working order and the road between A and B doesn't have too many hills along it. So before you rush out and throw cash at your dealer, ask around your friends and family and find out whether they've got an abandoned bike taking up space in the garage or garden shed. Pump up the tyres, ride it around a quiet road and if it feels good give it a service and adopt it as Your First Bike. It will allow you to find out whether cycling really is for you before you spend too much hard-earned cash, and to make a more informed decision about what kind of bike suits you when (or if) you do.

That said, the more you cycle, the more you'll appreciate a bike that's suited to your needs. The riding position, the gearing, the weight and the wheel size are just some of the features that vary between models, along, of course, with the style and the level of quality you're looking for.

where should I buy from?

Bikes are often sold at a discount online. You'll click to choose, and a few days later a humungous cardboard box will arrive at your house, containing a partially assembled bike.

The savings may be tempting, but resist. There are some very good reasons for buying at a local bike shop, and the price difference may not even be that great. You'll get all the staff's expertise and advice, the option of a test ride, a fully assembled bike and likely a free service in a few weeks – the cables will stretch a little, so the brakes and gears may need adjusting to be fully safe. It should also be the start of a beautiful relationship. There will soon come a time when your mechanic is your bike's best friend.

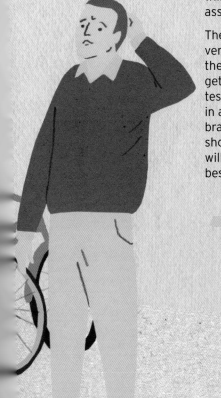

it's all in the fit

Bikes come in different frame sizes. The key measurement is taken up the seat tube from the centre of the bottom bracket and may run the full length of the seat tube, to the junction with the top tube, or on bikes with a top tube sloping down from front to back, the point where the top tube would hit the seat tube, if the top tube was horizontal and the seat tube was long enough. Confusing, huh? Plus, there are lots more nuances. Is it measured in inches or centimetres? To the edge of a tube or the middle? And, for road bikes, the horizontal distance from seat tube to head tube is also important.

Some people love all this. For them, there is plenty of pleasure to be had pondering manufacturers' charts and diagrams that plot bike size against height and inside leg. If you are not among them, rely instead on the advice of your bike dealer and remember that frame size isn't the whole story.

A comfortable fit is also about the position and height of the saddle and handlebars, which are much easier and cheaper to adjust after purchase.

bike frame anatomy

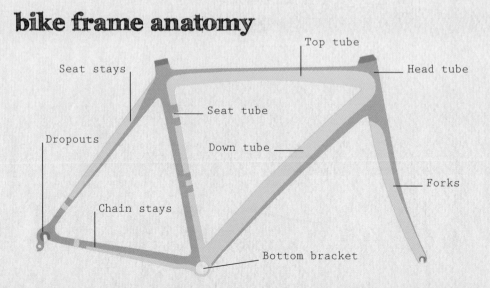

As a general rule, when your leg is at its fullest extent in the pedal stroke, it should still have a bit of flex in it. And when you stand with one foot on either side of the bike, you should have a couple of centimetres of clearance over the top tube; double that if you plan to ride off road.

While we're on frames, you'll hear a lot about bike geometry, and how racy or relaxed it is. Bike geometry can be really fascinating but it's a bit of a specialist subject, so, again, rely on your dealer's advice, and avoid sporty geometry unless you are a sporty rider: what's responsive and aerodynamic in a race is unstable and uncomfortable on a commute.

FRAME MATERIALS

STEEL
Pumped: Durable and good value.
Puncture: Can be a bit heavy, but go for well-made Chromoly tubing and you should be fine, or better than fine at the top end

ALUMINIUM
Pumped: Light but tubes need to be quite fat to keep it strong. A nice ride on smooth terrain…
Puncture:… but you'll feel every bump on rougher roads

TITANIUM
Pumped: Sooo beautiful, sooo light, sooo durable…
Puncture:… sooo expensive

CARBON FIBRE
Pumped: Light, smooth and state of the art
Puncture: It's the least durable frame material and may not survive a crash

hybrids

Hybrids are great all-rounders. They combine the larger wheels and light build of a road bike with the shape and off-road resilience of a mountain bike. Flat handlebars allow you to sit tall in the saddle, giving a good view of the road, and mean that you have all your controls – steering, brakes, gears and bell – within easy reach. They have a wide range of gears to get you up and down hills and some comfort kit like a cushioned saddle and mudguard fittings.

Good for: Commuters who like to get up a bit of speed and also short to medium recreational rides at weekends, on roads and easy trails.
Not for: Specialists, stylists.

road bikes

Road bikes are designed to perform well on paved roads, whether for commuting, touring, club rides, sportives or racing. The exact set-up depends on the use, but they all have lightweight wheels, drop handlebars, derailleur gears and, if you're prepared to pay for them, lightweight frame and components. The drop handlebars result in an aerodynamic stretched-out position, which is more comfortable than it looks, with the option of several different hand positions. Touring bikes will have more gears and more fittings on the frame for utilities like racks, mudguards and bottle cages – make sure you don't accidentally buy a bike that's too sporty for your needs and lacks these.

Good for: Efficient performance, classic style options.
Not for: Nervous first-timers.

dutch bikes

If it's reliability, practicality and solidity you're after, then the Dutch-style bike is for you. Inspired by the workhorse steeds of Amsterdam and a century's worth of utility riding worldwide, they have a distinctly retro look. They're upright, with high handlebars that may curve round to the side, and step-through frames, to avoid that vulgar business of getting your leg up and over. Dutch bikes bristle with features designed to make cycling fit easily into your life, rather than the other way round, such as chain guards, stands, built-in locks, baskets or carrying racks, dynamo lights and low-maintenance hub gears. And if they don't go so very fast, then at least they won't make you all sweaty, either.

Good for: People who don't like cycling to be a lifestyle.
Not for: Anyone in too much of a hurry.

single-speeds/ fixed-wheels

A single-speed bike is, as you might expect, a bike with just one gear. It's cycling at its simplest and most satisfying. No gears means less weight to carry, less to think about, less to look after and less to go wrong. Result! Of course, that one gear has to take you everywhere, but if you're a reasonably fit person cycling on reasonably flat terrain, odds are it will.

A fixed-wheel bike, or 'fixie', is a single-speed with no freewheel – which means that if you stop pedalling, the back wheel will stop revolving (and it might not want to). It takes practice to master a safe technique, but it's worth it for the thrill of direct control.

Good for: Couriers, purists, hipsters and lovers of vintage bikes (often converted into single speeds).
Not for: Hilly streets, and fixies aren't for beginners.

MORE BEST BIKE BUYS

FOR OLDER LEGS
An electric bike (e-bike)

FOR RAIL COMMUTERS
A folding bike

FOR TALKATIVE TOURERS
A recumbent
(lying-down bike)

FOR SMALL BUSINESSES
A delivery bike

FOR HAPPY COUPLES
A tandem

FOR TODDLERS
A push-along bike

FOR LOVERS OF BIKE CRAFT
A cycle hand-made from scratch

mountain bikes

The clue's in the name – mountain bikes are designed for use off road, and not just on gentle tracks but on steep, rocky slopes, too, in all weather. They have super-grippy tyres designed to handle everything from mud soup to slickrock, lots of low-end gears for tough climbs and sometimes smaller wheels than road bikes for strength and control. Rough riding rattles your bones – to cushion the impact, MTBs often have front suspension, and sometimes rear suspension, too. All these mountain features can slow you down on paved roads, so consider a mountain bike only if you plan to do some serious off-roading. It's thrilling, companionable and not a little hardcore.

Good for: Sport and recreational MTB, expedition touring.
Not for: Commuting by road.

dream machines

Serious cyclists fall in love with the state-of-the-art design and sheer speed of top-end machines – the kind of bikes the pros ride. Made to sleek aerodynamic designs, with the lightest, most advanced components, they combine precision handling with the kind of power transfer that only envelope-pushing engineering can deliver. You buy a bike like this for competition and serious training – but you may well want to stay on it all the time. It might cost more than a month's salary, but that's still a lot less than a sports car.

Good for: Middle-aged men.
Not for: Anyone who doesn't know the difference between titanium and uranium.

gears and brakes

You can spend a month's salary on a top-of-the-line frame and wheels – but your bike can ride like a donkey if you have a poor gearing set-up and dodgy brakes.

gears

Derailleurs Most modern bikes are sold with a derailleur gearing system, with two or three chainrings at the front (by the pedals) and a cassette with multiple sprockets on the rear wheel. Bikes with derailleur gears come with two gear shifters, usually mounted on the handlebars – one to move the chain between the front chainrings, the other to shunt it between the rear sprockets. Your selection of front chainring and rear sprocket combine to form your gear, which determines how much wellie you have to put into pedalling. More gears isn't necessarily better – the important thing is the spread between the highest and the lowest. Derailleur gears require a bit of maintenance, but they're versatile, reliable and affordable.

Hub gears The clue's in the name: hub gear mechanics are contained within the rear wheel's hub, so you just need one chainring at the front and a single sprocket at the back. Hub gears are heavier and more expensive than derailleurs, but they're extremely reliable and require virtually no maintenance – ideal for a touring bike or an around-town workhorse.

Single-speed and fixed-wheel bikes Single-speed and fixed-wheel set-ups have just a single gear – a chainring at the front, a sprocket at the back, and no mechanics inside the hub. If you live somewhere flat and are making shortish journeys, this low-maintenance, low-cost option is well worth considering.

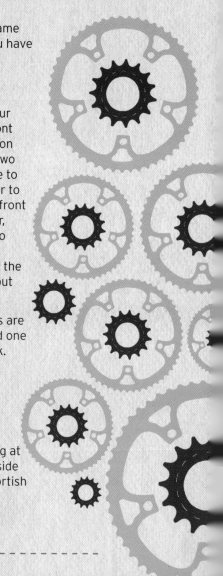

brakes

Rim brakes Rim brakes are the most common type of bike brake. They're connected to the brake lever by a cable; squeeze the lever and the brake pads close around the rim of the wheel, slowing the bike. Rim brakes come in a variety of styles – callipers, cantilevers, roller-cams and more – but the principle remains the same. They're a bit less effective in the wet, but they're cheap, easy to maintain and reliable.

Disc brakes Disc brakes consist of a metal disc attached to the wheel hub, with brake pads mounted next to the disc. They're heavier and more expensive than rim brakes but offer more reliable stopping power in all weathers, so they're popular on mountain bikes and everyday hybrids.

WHAT'S A GROUPSET?

In a nutshell, a groupset consists of those bike parts that mean you can move (crankset, chain, chainrings, cassette, gear shifters, derailleurs, bottom bracket) and stop (brakes, pads, levers). They're marketed and fitted as complete sets. Your bike shop can explain the differences between groupsets – but as a rule, the more you pay, the smoother your gearing, the more reliable your braking, and the lighter your bike.

Kitting yourself out

Here's a secret: if you don't like luminous, stretchy cycle kit, you don't have to wear it. Riding a bike isn't like going into outer space: no special suit is required. The only real wardrobe considerations to ponder are:

• **Will it get stuck in the machinery?** This is bad both for the clothing, which will get dirty and may tear, and also for you and the bike, which may come to an abrupt and dangerous halt. Tuck away trailing laces, belts and scarves and restrain flapping trouser legs with a clip or band.

• **Will it be embarrassing?** Skirts ride up, trousers ride down, necklines offer a different view if you're down on the handlebars. Fitted skirts are a no-no on a bike with a crossbar.

• **Will I overheat?** Depending how fast you ride, you will warm up quite a lot en route, especially in the summer. You'll generally need one layer less than you would as a pedestrian, but you'll also need to protect yourself from the weather.

• **Will I get cold?** Riding exposes you to wind chill, because of your speed. Gloves and a hat or skullcap are advisable in winter.

BRIEFS ENCOUNTER

There's no need to wear underwear with padded cycle shorts or tights; in fact, you're better off without it. Honest. It just means more things to rub up the wrong way.

• **Will it keep me dry?** Rain can hit at any time, and nothing is more annoying than having to abandon your bike.

If you choose to ride in street clothes, you can get away with buying just a cycle clip and a rain jacket, especially on a town bike. But lots of people prefer bike-specific kit. It's cut to be comfortable, and offers useful features.

legwear

The main feature of cycle shorts and tights is the padding. Saddle comfort is a very personal thing but lots of riders find this helps, especially on longer rides. Shorts can be tight or loose with an insert to hold the padding in place, and come up high on the back to cover your kidneys.

cycle shirts

Cycle-specific shirts (or 'jerseys') are cut to fit the leaning-forward riding position, with a long back and arms. They are made in fabrics that 'wick away' perspiration, and may have long front zips and underarm vents for more ventilation. Other rider-pleasing features include easy-grip zip tags, back pockets for day-ride kits and phone pockets.

helmets

The most important thing about your helmet is that it does its job. It needs to be specific to cycling (don't 'borrow' your ski or skateboard lid), new (so you can be sure it hasn't been damaged by past knocks), and to conform to safety standards. After that, the most important thing is that you like it enough to want to put it on. Choose a style that appeals and, if you like to ride fast, ensure that it's well ventilated (or your head will get uncomfortably hot). Ask your dealer to help adjust it correctly – a badly fitting helmet is worse than none at all. It needs to be set straight on the head and fastened securely but not too tightly under the chin.

You can buy fleecy and windproof skullcaps to wear alone or under your helmet in winter. Race caps, beloved by riders enamoured of racing culture, can also be worn under your lid.

rain jacket

The point of a jacket is to avoid getting wet, but you need to balance protecting yourself from rain against trapping the moisture and warmth your own body generates. The term 'breathable' refers to fabrics that 'wick away' perspiration but don't let water in. There's no such thing as a perfectly breathable, perfectly waterproof jacket, and some riders prefer one that's only showerproof and windproof, but does a good job of wicking. A good jacket is your most important piece of clothing, and is worth splashing out on. Look for reflective trim in sensible places and a streamlined, comfortable fit, especially at the collar and cuffs, and remember that the vulnerable points are the zip and seams (including rear pockets).

cycle shoes

You can cycle in any shoes – even with heels – as long as they don't slide off the pedals, but some people prefer cycle-specific shoes, which come with cleats that clip into a fitting on special pedals. Many riders love the secure positioning, direct connection to the drive and increased efficiency, but others dislike feeling 'trapped' (as you need to unclip before you can put a foot down). Look for recessed cleats if you want to wear cycle shoes all day.

more useful kit

Waterproof trousers: in case you have to ride through a downpour... **Cycle gloves:** the padding can really help stop arm and shoulder pain from vibration... **A windproof gilet:** packs small and protects your core... **Arm warmers:** good for chilly mornings – peel them off when the sun comes out... **Thermal base layers:** for cold-weather rides... **Overshoes:** to keep your feet dry and toasty.

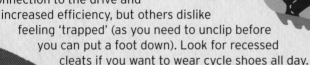

Bicycle bits

Buying a bike is a serious business given the cash involved, but you can have some fun accessorizing it.

ting ting!

Glamorous, no. Potentially life-saving, yes. The bike bell is the universally accepted polite way of letting pedestrians and other riders know that they're in your path. They come in a variety of styles, including classic clangers, tiny ones for drop handlebars and novelty ones with compasses and the like. Some riders prefer a horn - definitely louder, but not quite as civil.

wicker men (and women)

You can pack your stuff in a backpack or courier bag, but if you prefer to let your bike take the strain, build in some on-board carrying capacity. Front baskets are the convenient choice if you ride a sit-up-straight bike and want to be able to sling you stuff in and go. The wire or wicker type are the most convenient, but their obvious drawback is that they're open to the elements, so you might prefer a modern waterproof bar bag. Either way, make sure it's firmly attached.

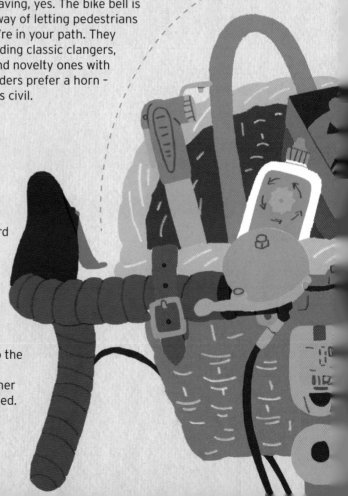

load it up

To carry larger loads out of the weather, you'll need panniers, larger bags that fit onto a rack (that you'll also need to purchase). For everyday riding and shorter tours, rear panniers will be enough (you can always tie extras on to the rack with bungees).

Classic panniers have capacious interiors and outer pockets. You can also get fully waterproof panniers with roll-down closures, but no pockets; commuters might prefer a briefcase-style rack bag (some have padding for laptops) and shoppers, a pretty holdall. On all, look out for robust construction and secure rack fittings.

drink me

Even on a short fun ride you should drink regularly. Fit a bottle cage to your frame, slot in a water bottle, and you'll be able to rehydrate without having to stop. It makes sense to have at least one bottle, and two for longer rides or warmer days. (They're easy to take off.)

easy keysy

QR (quick release) skewers allow you to take your wheels off quickly and easily - really handy if you need to repair a puncture on the road. The only trouble is that they also allow thieves to take your wheels off quickly and easily, so be sure to secure both wheels when you park. Alternatively, buy special QR skewers with locks (also an option for removable saddles, or you could just bolt them on).

GIRLS, GIRLS, GIRLS

Just in case you hadn't noticed, women are a different shape from men. And not just in the bumpy areas, but in their proportions: they tend to have longer legs and shorter torsos. So one common bike upgrade for girls is a shorter stem to bring the handlebars closer. As for clothing, it's all in the fit: curvy women, especially, will appreciate a custom cut (if not the lack of pockets). If shorts aren't your thing, look out for 'skorts' instead, or go retro with bloomers.

bright ideas

Be seen, be safe. Even if you ride in a well-lit city, you need to be visible in the dark, and visible from a distance, too, so that drivers can plan to avoid you in plenty of time. Bicycle lights and reflectors are compulsory in some parts of the world, and advisable everywhere.

Front lights have two purposes: to alert other road users to your presence, and to light your way ahead. Make sure yours are visible from the side, as well as the front, to motorists turning out of side streets. Lighting and battery technology is moving fast, and you can buy LED lights strong enough to illuminate your path on night rides, even when there's no moon. (Awesome.) Cute, tiny clip-on lights are great as extra illumination, but don't rely on them as your main light, even in town.

Rear lights are there to let people behind you know that you're there, so they usually have attention-grabbing flash modes.

Batteries last ages in LED lights, but when they go, they go quickly, so replace them as soon as they look dim. Now you can also buy battery-free LEDs that charge via USB.

Reflective areas on bike, bags and clothing are an effective way of signalling your presence to motorists in the dark. Some riders also like to make sure that they are unmissable day and night by dressing from head to toe in high-visibility clothing, from fluoro helmet and backpack cover, to luminous cycle clips.

lock, stock and barrel

Sadly, bicycle theft is common, particularly in cities. The first thing to know about bike locks is that none of them are foolproof, and they shouldn't be your only line of defence. Always leave your bike somewhere busy and well lit, preferably where a getaway vehicle would have trouble parking and ideally where you can keep an eye on it. Register it online (the police can advise, and may also fit an electronic tag), and note down the frame number (so it can be returned to you if the culprits are caught).

Use a D-lock to attach the frame and back wheel of your bike to something immovable, preferably a stand (and definitely not a traffic sign). If you are prepared to carry the weight, attach the front wheel separately with another, smaller D-lock; if not, run a cable to it from the first lock, or remove it and slot it into the back lock.

Buy the fattest, heaviest D-lock you can afford (chains are not as secure), in the minimum size you need (to allow as little leverage as possible).

HIP TIP

Don't carry your D-lock on your belt. If you skid, you may fall on it and cause your hip serious damage.

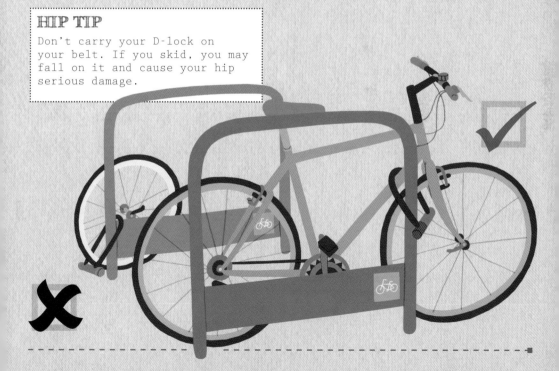

add-ons and upgrades

When you buy a bike, choose the best frame and groupset you can afford. The other parts can be changed relatively cheaply for something that suits you better. Do it at the time of purchase and you might be able to work out a deal.

tyres

Want brightly coloured tyres? Reinforced tyres for puncture protection? A luminous sidewall? Or just a better ride? Now's your chance. Tyres keep your bike safely attached to the ground in all weathers and on all surfaces. Models designed for off-road use – usually fat and knobbly – will have more traction than you'll need on tarmac, and you'll have to pedal harder for no good reason. Change them to 'slick' tyres instead. Road tyres have varying grips for different weather – make sure yours are right for where you ride.

saddles

If you know what kind of saddle suits you, lucky you. Saddle comfort is a really personal thing, and it depends not just on the type of saddle but its position, angle and distance from the pedals and handlebars. Carry an Allen key with you and keep tweaking until you nail the perfect set-up.

Looks are deceptive when it comes to saddles. The sofa-like ones can be a bit bulky and chafe, while the scary-looking blades might be all you need if you have a narrow pelvis (as most men do). Lots of people swear by old-style leather saddles that mould themselves to fit you, and some women find that saddles split into two 'wings' give their derrières a new lease of life.

AFTER

mudguards

Racers hate them for ruining their bike's lines, and everyone hates them when they rattle and rub. But there's no denying that mudguards do an important job in the wet: stopping muddy road water splashing a 'skunk stripe' on your back and gunging up the moving parts. Get the shop to put them on unless you're confident: it's a fiddly job.

pedals

The main reason to replace pedals is to fit clipless pedals (or, if you're nervous, pedals with clips on one side and a standard platform on the other). At the least, screw on toe clips, which help keep your feet in position and make for a better stroke.

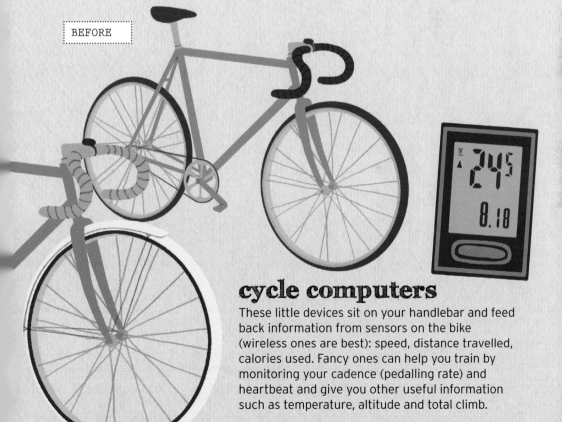

BEFORE

cycle computers

These little devices sit on your handlebar and feed back information from sensors on the bike (wireless ones are best): speed, distance travelled, calories used. Fancy ones can help you train by monitoring your cadence (pedalling rate) and heartbeat and give you other useful information such as temperature, altitude and total climb.

Easy riding

We're figuring you can probably ride a bike already. Once you've mastered the magic trick of staying upright, pedalling and steering all at the same time, it's for life. But to get the most fun, speed and safety out of your time in the saddle, it's useful to understand a little about the physics and mechanics of the bicycle, and develop your technique accordingly.

pedalling

Your pedal stroke is your bike's motor, so it's worth making it as efficient as possible. Experiment with the height of your saddle, and slide it forwards or backwards along its rails, until your stroke feels strong and comfortable.

Pedal with the ball of your foot, not your toes or instep. Keep your heel down and imagine yourself pushing down towards the 5 o'clock position of the revolution. At this point your legs should be at their most extended but still have a little flex. Aim for a continuous circular motion rather than piston strokes and if you have clip-in shoes or toe clips use them to help draw the pedal back up.

position

If you're riding into the wind or want to make the most of a fast downhill, bend down low over the handlebars to minimise wind resistance. For steep climbs, keep your weight forwards and stand up on the pedals for a last push. Standing up also helps cushion you on bumpy terrain (or potholes); just let your legs act as shock absorbers.

brakes

Try and use your brakes as little as possible - plan ahead instead. It's better to 'feather' your brakes to reduce speed, for example on a descent, than jam them on. Never apply your back brakes without also using your front brakes, or vice versa.

gears

Riding around town, you'll probably only need to use one or two gears. But choose those gears carefully. It's better to pedal quickly in a lower gear than to pedal slowly in a high gear. Your knees will thank you, and you'll be faster off the blocks.

Gears come into their own on out-of-town rides when there are lots of ups and downs. The lower gears will allow you to get up hills smoothly without going into cardio overdrive, and the higher ones to keep the momentum going down slopes and onto the flat.

A BIT RUSTY?

If you haven't ridden as an adult, or want to try out a new type of bike or technique, find some empty tarmac in your local park and practise your moves safely away from traffic. You could follow the court markings of a basketball court to perfect your steering, or ride alongside a railing if you need something to hold on to.

cornering

Perfecting your cornering technique is useful even on short rides: it will keep you stable and holding a predictable line. If there's space, take a wide approach. Stop pedalling and brake as you prepare and take the corner with your inside pedal at the top of its stroke. If you're going fast enough to feel a bit of centrifugal force, lean your body slightly into the corner.

road sense

In town, you'll be sharing the tarmac with other road users of all stripes, in an intricate ballet of different needs and speeds. You need to ride both safely and responsibly, and this takes some practice.

Familiarize yourself with the local highway code. It may set legal standards for the roadworthiness of your bike, require lighting or helmets, forbid riding when inebriated and stipulate bike-specific laws. Your local riders' association will also have plenty of helpful advice.

Cycling laws, conventions and infrastructure vary from country to country, even city to city. In some South American cities, for example, going the 'wrong' way down one-way streets ('salmoning') is accepted as a good way to stay visible – in New York it's highly controversial. But the following basic riding techniques hold good everywhere.

- **Don't ride in the gutter** - stay a good metre (3 ft) from the kerb or parked cars, and more if the situation requires it. It's up to the traffic behind you to pass when it's safe – you have just as much of a right to be there as they do.
- **Before any manoeuvre, look behind you.** Practise doing this safely and quickly on both sides. Some riders like to use a mirror – bike specific ones are available.
- **Indicate both left and right turns** clearly by putting your arm out horizontally.
- **If you are going straight on at a junction,** or passing a turn-off, check the car behind isn't about to cut you up as it turns, and that no cars are emerging into your path.
- **At advance cycle stop boxes,** riders can wait at red lights ahead of traffic rather than getting stuck among it. Allow riders behind you access these areas as well.

LONG, TALL AND DANGEROUS TO KNOW

Long vehicles, particularly lorries and trucks, are the biggest danger to cyclists, and cause many fatalities. Their turning circle is broad and unpredictable and can cut off the corner on the inside, trapping a cyclist against railings or even under the truck's own wheels. The driver in the elevated cab, has very limited visibility, and cannot see directly ahead, directly behind or fully down either side. Never shimmy up the side of a long vehicle, even if there's a bike path, and don't trust their indicators, whether on or off.

- **If you can ride** at the same speed as a car in urban traffic, you may prefer to take up a place in the centre of the lane.

If all this seems daunting, consider taking cycle classes, which are widely available and very confidence-building. And if you have a wobbly moment or feel vulnerable, just get off and walk.

Cycling safely is as much about where you ride as how you ride. For advice on finding the best route, see pages 40-41.

staying safe

The key to staying safe in traffic is to remember that drivers, insulated in their little metal boxes, don't always see cyclists properly or know how to behave around them – how much space they need, or what they are likely to do next. They may make sudden moves or forget to indicate or check their mirrors. Road architecture and signage are generally designed for motor vehicles rather than human-powered ones. Drivers tend to think the streets are theirs.

Samurai have nothing on city cyclists, who need to maintain a permanent state of alertness, achieve 360° vision and calculate and re-calculate risks – all while keeping a clear head and still, hopefully, enjoying the ride. After a while this becomes second nature, but you should never relax too much, even in a bike lane. Never go so fast you can't stop within your line of sight, always leave time and space for the unexpected and don't take chances – the sad fact is that riders tend to come off worse not only in encounters with other vehicles, but with pedestrians, too. Try and make eye contact with drivers during your moves and use your bell or just call out politely to pedestrians (and give way to them on shared paths).

Accidents aren't always caused by collisions. Have your bike serviced regularly to ensure a brake doesn't fail or a cable snap at a key moment, and make sure you're not trailing anything that can get stuck in the wheels or gears.

If you see a white-painted memorial bicycle, say a silent goodbye to a fallen rider and a thank-you to friends and relatives who have put it there to mark the danger spot.

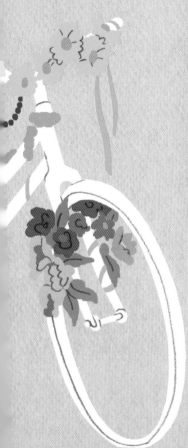

use your head

Wearing a helmet helps protect your head from impacts, but it doesn't turn you into a superhero. Helmets don't stop accidents from happening, and motorists may take more risks around lid-wearers. And of course it's not only your head that could be damaged by a close encounter with a vehicle. So if you use a helmet, don't let it lull you into a false sense of security – stay just as alert as a bare-headed rider.

HAZARDS TO WATCH FOR

- Car doors opening (always allow space)
- Pedestrians with headphones on, particularly runners – they won't hear your bell (best not to wear them yourself, either)
- Pedestrians stepping off the kerb or crossing roads through slow-moving traffic without looking
- Drivers on the phone or invisible behind tinted windows
- Potholes, ice patches, wet leaves, broken glass and puddles so deep you can't see the bottom
- Rubbish collectors – beware flying bin bags
- Cyclists moving into your path as you pass
- Dogs – they do like a nice chase

life cycle

Cycling isn't just a convenient, cheap, healthy and generally brilliant means of getting from A to B. It's a culture all of its own, complete with subcultures and a sneaky habit of taking over your life, from local activism to fun stuff to do at the weekend. Meet a fellow cyclist at a party and you'll leave with a new friend.

in the saddle

As well as going on social rides (see page 58), you could pick up a mallet and learn to play high-adrenaline bicycle polo; go on a treasure hunt or out geocaching; get even fitter by getting serious about spinning; do a fun ride like a 'Tour de Donut' (there are several in the USA) or London's famous folding bike race; or even help pedal-power a film screening.

in the community

Cycling, being an all-round Good Thing, is at the heart of lots of charity, environmental and community organisations. Your local cycling club will always be glad of volunteer ride leaders; you could sign on to teach children how to ride (or organize a fun 'bike rodeo' for them); or learn maintenance skills with a charity that fixes bikes and ships them to Africa. At grass-roots level, there's still a lot of lobbying to be done for improved cycling facilities, or you could start a bicycle users' group at work.

out shopping

Here's a warning: buying cycle gear can become a costly hobby, but it can also be very enjoyable. There's a whole world of designers and craftspeople making clever things for the bike, or you can buy second-hand and develop a satisfying vintage habit. You might even end up building up your own bike.

in your datebook

Cyclists are a friendly and social bunch. (Some of those weekend events are more party than pedalling.) If you're new to an area or want to expand your social circle, you'll find the local club very welcoming, and if you've an aching heart, there are several dating websites just for riders. Cycle cafés welcome all comers, and are a good place to find out what's going on.

from your armchair

Cycle sport can become compulsive viewing with, long, multi-stage team races like the Tour de France, Vuelta a España and Giro D'Italia developing into dramatic sagas, complete with thrills and spills, heroes, villains and vendettas. Cycle-racing is like football or baseball: its history still resonates – it's more than just a sport.

Planning your routes

commuting

It's worth investing some time in planning your commute. Your usual driving or bus route might be the shortest way in, but it's likely to be a traffic-filled main road. A quieter, back-street journey might be longer but will be safer and more enjoyable, and possibly quicker, too.

Start by finding out about official cycle routes. Your local cycling association will have maps of these; many now show up on Google Maps. Some will be dedicated lanes on main highways, some just quiet side streets; some will go through parks and along waterways; and some – the really fun ones – are special cycle roads, whether purpose-built or converted from old railways, etc. Also, take a look at pedalling.com in the USA and sustrans.org in the UK. Mark your best guess at a route on a map and test it out one quiet Sunday. Remember that one-way systems might mean you have to come a different way home. If you need to consult your map, pull off out of the way of traffic. A paper map or marked-up printout is most reliable, though a smartphone or tablet is a useful backup.

what makes a good ride?

It's good to feel a sense of accomplishment, by exploring somewhere you've never been before, making a full circuit of a park or lake, following a river or visiting a landmark, for example. You can theme your rides – plan a coffee shop circuit, a spring-flower spy mission or a tour of historic buildings. And always plan in a refreshment or picnic stop.

afternoons out

For short leisure rides, again start with official cycle routes. Pin the maps up on your wall and highlight planned and completed routes (you can log these in your Journal, too). Visit the websites of local country parks to find out if they have any cycle trails. Ask your friends where they ride and sign up to local cycling blogs.

If some or all of your ride is on standard roads, choose quiet ones; if main roads are unavoidable for short stretches, look at satellite mapping to see how wide they are and whether there's a pavement you can push bikes along.

You'll soon find out how far you like to ride, and how fast. If you plan your first ride at 16-24 km (10-15 miles), and allow two hours (not including stops), odds are you'll be pleasantly surprised by how easy it feels.

BIKE BUDDIES

If you're nervous about riding to work, find a workmate who lives near you and ask if you can cycle in with them.

longer rides

Planning longer rides can become a military operation, with checkpoints and numbered turn lists. It's harder to get lost now GPS-equipped smartphones can locate you in an instant, but equally, it's better not to go wrong in the first place – after all, who wants to backtrack up a lovely long descent that's flipped into a gruelling climb? – and phone signals do have a habit of going AWOL when you need them most. It's fun to pore over maps to devise your own routes and then see how they work out in real life, but if it's not your thing, go out on organized or waymarked rides instead.

Follow the advice given for planning afternoons out (see page 41), but also bear in mind:

- **Exit strategy** Bad weather or a tired rider might mean you want to cut your ride short. Try and plan in alternative ways home (perhaps by train).
- **Total ascent** Be aware how much climbing the route includes, and set it against the abilities of your group. You might want some stiff ascents to improve your fitness, or you might want to keep things nice and level.
- **Water on hot days.** Include a stop to refill your water bottles if you're not taking a meal break.
- **Details, details** Read your map's key carefully and make sure your route will work on the ground. If your chosen road appears to cross a highway, make sure it doesn't in fact dead-end; if it follows a path or track, check it's legal to ride on; and if you're on road bikes, it's best avoid paths and unmade roads altogether, unless they're cycle-specific.

Take a map with you, the larger-scale the better, but aim to ride from a list of route directions that don't take as long to consult.

HI-TECH HELP

Garmin makes handlebar-mounted devices especially designed for cycling. They offer typical cycle computer features, along with GPS and built-in digital maps and can do some really clever stuff along the lines of planning and recording your rides and helping you train. You can also download smartphone apps that do some of the same things - they're a lot cheaper, but not as well-specced for the bike. Both give you really handy elevation profiles and also allow you to share your routes with other people (and ride theirs, too), as do the websites bikely.com and mapmyride.com.

Tech talk

Bikes are trusty steeds that don't take very much looking after, but you do need to keep the drivetrain clean and lubricated and be alert to things that can go wrong. Book a service at least once a year (keep a record in your Journal), use our troubleshooting checklist and listen out for any strange clicks and whirs. A little bit of ongoing maintenance is within everyone's reach, especially if you get to know your bike and learn to use the adjusters on the gears and brakes (ask your dealer or mechanic).

the right tool for the job

A basic home toolkit should include:

- **Multitool** These pleasing penknives-for-bikes typically include some hexagonal Allen keys in various sizes, straight and cross-head screwdrivers and some spanners, plus some fancier bits.
- **Allen keys** You may want to get individual Allen keys for bolts you use often or are in a tricky place for a multitool.
- **Adjustable spanner** Plus a pedal spanner and one for getting your wheels off if they're not QR.
- **Pliers** Needle-nosed ones for cabling and fine adjustments, blunter ones for general gripping.
- **Pump** Get a small one to take out with you and a floor (track) pump for super-easy inflation at home. A pressure gauge is really useful.
- **For cleaning** Degreaser, general cleaner, old toothbrushes, sponge, rags.
- **For puncture repair** Tyre levers (two or three), puncture repair kit, spare inner tubes (make sure you get the right size and valve).
- **Bottle opener** Because it'll be a lot more fun with a beer.

it's not just hot air!

The one bike fix that everyone can do is also the one that makes the most difference to your ride. Keep your tyres well pumped up and your bike will fly along with much less effort. If you ride mainly on smooth surfaces, fill to close to maximum capacity (marked on the sidewall); go for a slightly lower pressure if you need a bit more cushioning.

There are two types of tyre valve: a fat one (Schrader) and a thin one (Presta). Presta valves have a tiny screw at the top that you need to undo carefully before pumping. Be sure to tighten again afterwards.

TROUBLESHOOTING

Make these checks every few weeks and before any long ride.

Easy to do at home

Fairly easy to do at home, once you know how

Best left to a specialist

☐ Tyre pressure low.
ACTION: pump up

☐ Check tyre tread hasn't worn down too much and look for cracks, deep cuts and embedded road debris.
ACTION: fit a new tyre

☐ Loose spokes.
ACTION: tighten spokes and re-true wheel if necessary

☐ Wheels not running straight and true.
ACTION: check wheel is tight in the dropouts; if problem persists, take to mechanic

☐ Brake pads worn.
ACTION: replace

☐ Brakes not coming on when levers fully pulled.
ACTION: tighten cables using adjusters on the lever

☐ Brakes not coming on effectively.
ACTION: could be several things. Some adjustments are easy, but if in doubt, take to mechanic or

☐ Gear changes not smooth.
ACTION: you may be able to adjust this yourself using the limit screws. If not, take to mechanic or

☐ Chain slipping or coming off.
ACTION: take to mechanic

☐ Cables fraying.
ACTION: replacing cables is easy to learn, but until you're confident, take to mechanic

punctures sorted

You're bowling along and suddenly it feels like you're rolling on your wheel rims. That's a fast puncture. Stop and get off the bike before any damage is done. It's taxi time (or roadside-repair time for the well equipped).

You could have sworn you pumped up your tyre only yesterday, but now it's really soft again. That's a slow puncture. If there's a bit of air left in it, ride gently home or to a bike shop.

Everyone gets a few punctures every year. Just as well they're really easy to fix.

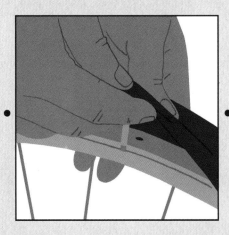

1 Turn the bike upside down and remove the offending wheel. You may have to release the brake. Let any remaining air out, then dig a tyre lever under the rim near the valve and lever the tyre off. Click the hook at the end of the lever onto a spoke and repeat a little further along using another tyre lever, then again. The tyre will soon come loose. Release it using a lever, then run your fingers around the tyre feeling for anything sharp.

2 Take the cap and retaining ring off the valve and push it through the hole in the rim, then pull the whole inner tube out. To put the new tube in, remove the cap, push the valve into place and secure the retaining ring.

PERFECT PATCHING

Don't waste the old inner tube. You'll probably be able to fix it. Find the puncture by submerging the tube in water while pumping in air. A trail of bubbles will lead to the damage. If it's substantial, chuck the tube; otherwise, draw a big 'X' to mark the spot with a waterproof marker. Dry the area around it and abrade it gently with sandpaper. Apply rubber solution, leave for a minute or so until nearly dry, then press on a patch, hold, and peel off the backing.

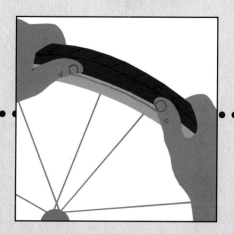

3 Inflate the tube slightly, then seat it on the rim under the tyre, working in alternate directions away from the valve. Then push the edge of the tyre back under the rim.

4 This can get tough at the end. If your thumbs aren't strong enough to stretch the last segment over, holler for help the first time and then invest in a special tool (don't use tyre levers). Put the wheel back on the bike (reassembling the brake if necessary), turn it over and pump the tyre up fully.

clean machine

You want to keep your bicycle pristine because it's your pride and joy – and also because dirt can damage the working parts. Try to clean it every couple of weeks, especially in wet weather. If you go on muddy off-road rides, wash your bike as soon as you get home.

For a general clean, a sunny day, a sponge, some spray-on bike cleaner or detergent and a gentle hosepipe are all you need. Take your bike outside and get to work on the loose dirt with a brush, then apply the cleaner, put your wellies on and have some fun with sponge and water.

A bike's drivetrain – that's the chainrings, chain, derailleurs, jockey wheels and cassette (or the sprocket on a single-speed or hub-geared bike) – tends to pick up road dirt and mash it into a black paste, which not only leaves oily tattoos on your legs but erodes the working parts. It's not the easiest thing in the word to get rid of, but you'll really notice the difference in the ride after a clean-and-lube.

IT'S A DIRTY JOB...

... But someone's got to do it. That someone doesn't have to be you, though. Some bike shops offer a valet service – worth considering if you don't like getting dirt under your fingernails.

To clean, turn your bike upside down on some old newspaper. With an old toothbrush, get rid of any obviously claggy bits. Take your chain off if you know how (you might need a tool, or be able to open a link) and clean it separately. Then spray some degreaser onto the moving parts, turn the pedals a few times (if the chain is still on) and get to work with the toothbrush again. You can buy special implements to clean between the sprockets on the cassette, or use strips of old T-shirt, which you'll also need to wipe everything down thoroughly, polishing off the grime.

grease is the word

Always lubricate the drive, or 'lube', as the pros say, after cleaning. Use a bike-specific product rather than a general-purpose oil. Drip it onto a section of chain, holding a rag underneath, then turn the pedals to expose a new section of chain and repeat. Turn the bike the right way up, and ask a friend to hold the back wheel off the ground and turn the pedals while you run through all the gears, front and back, to distribute the lube all around. Wipe off any excess.

Stretching your legs

It's the darnedest thing. If you just keep your legs going round, you'll find yourself going further and further. You've travelled ten miles in an hour, the sun's shining, you're enjoying the scenery and you're not even tired yet... It's hard for first-timers to believe, but once you've woken up your cycling muscles with commuting or a few short pleasure trips, 30-, 50- and 80-km (20-, 30- and 50-miles) rides really will be well within your reach – and your weekends will never be the same again.

A couple of provisos here. First, on longer rides you may well encounter the kind of climb that turns your face red and your language blue. Getting up these is great cardio training, but at first you'll need a low gear, a lot of patience and the chutzpah to get off and push if you have to. Second, if you choose to ride off-road, expect to cover shorter distances – rough terrain requires more energy.

As with most physical activity, it's a question of building things up gradually. A reasonably fit, occasional cyclist can expect to cover 50 km (30 miles) without too much suffering.

Do that on two successive weekends and then add about 8 km (5 miles) to your rides, going out every week or fortnight, and in two or three months, 80-100 km (50-62 miles) will feel easy, and you'll need to take fewer breaks. Your muscles might ache a bit the next day, but that will be nothing set against the fun you've had. Rolling through the landscape under your own power, alive to the seasons, leaving cares behind and feeling yourself getting fitter and stronger: these are the sublime pleasures of cycling.

It's at about this point that you may get properly bitten by the bug, and feel the need to hook up with your cycling brethren (and sistren). There's a whole world of cycling clubs out there running regular group rides and helping members develop their speed, skills and fitness. Join one that suits your level (some are recreational and some distinctly sporty) and you'll soon find yourself in a big, friendly peloton – team shirt and all.

MILEPOST ACHIEVEMENTS

- 30 km (20 miles)
- 50 km (30 miles)
- 64 km (40 miles)
- 80 km (50 miles)
- 100 km (62 miles)
- 120 km (75 miles)
- 161 km (100 miles)
- Mass ride
- Group/club ride
- Sportive/Gran Fondo/organized century
- Average speed of 24kph (15mph)
- Climb 30 m (1,000 ft) in a day
- Climb 1,000 m (3,280 ft) in a day
- Over 80 km (50 miles) two days running

ride further

Once you're happy riding around 50-60 km (30-40 miles) a day, whole new horizons hove into view. Link those days together, and you've got a cycling tour. Admittedly, touring takes a little more energy than a beach vacation, but it's uniquely suited to leisurely exploration and new discoveries. The medium pace of cycling is nicely balanced between seeing things close up and actually getting somewhere, and not being locked inside the private world of a car - you can connect with your surroundings with all your senses. Best of all, those local delicacies aren't an indulgence, but a perfectly legitimate calorie need.

tour planning

For your first tour, choose a not-too-mountainous area with towns and villages far enough apart for it to be attractive cycling country, but close enough together to be able to ride from one to another in a day, with lunch options. Consult a map to ensure there are enough back roads to escape heavy traffic. Wine country, remote coastlines, national parks and long-distance bike routes all qualify. Go outside your own back yard (perhaps to one of the world's famously cycling-friendly countries, such as France) and it will be a real voyage of discovery.

You'll need to do a little research to track down hotels that welcome cyclists and have off-street parking for your bikes. Also find out how busy they expect to be at that time of year: ideally, you want to book a hotel for the night that same morning, when you know how far you feel like riding and whether it's likely to rain. But equally, you don't want to risk being homeless for the night.

RIDING LIGHT
As a rule of thumb, pack everything you think you need for your ride, then unpack it, toss half of it aside and repack the rest. You'll need lots less than you think. You're powering the weight yourself.

team effort

One way to avoid any uncertainty is to book with a cycle holiday company, who will take care of all the arrangements and also carry your gear for you – plus they can pick you up in the 'sag wagon', if you can't pedal another mile. You'll benefit from the staff's language skills and local knowledge, and they will be able to lend bikes and do on-road repairs for you. For cycle tour companies, see page 63.

If you take your own bike, make sure you pack any spares that are unlikely to be easily available along your route.

ride faster

For many cyclists, a hobby soon develops into something a little sportier. They enjoy improving their physique and technique and so increasing their speed and endurance. The roads are one big outdoor gym, and the fitter they get the greater the scenic rewards. You don't have to be a Tour de France pro to be king of the mountains: the right gears and a pair of rock-hard calves will take any well-trained rider up into alpine peaks.

There's been an explosion recently in organized day rides that allow all-comers to challenge themselves and compete with other riders but that aren't, strictly speaking, races. Variously called sportives, randonnées and gran fondos, they are held on marked road routes, often closed to traffic. Riders are issued with a number and a chip that tracks their progress, and their times are published online. Demanding events over 62 km (100 miles) long with some punishing climbs (and names like 'the hell of the north' or 'death ride') are getting more popular, but shorter options are usually also offered, and there are gentler rides, too, for first timers. The results are classified by age and gender, so you can see how you compare against your peers.

If you find you really rather enjoy this kind of thing and might even be quite good at it, you could consider taking up cycling competitively. Cycle sport is friendly at grass roots level and, beyond the cost of the bike, not terribly expensive. Its various disciplines – BMX, mountain biking, road cycling (including time trials) and track cycling, not forgetting triathlon – have something for everybody. In fact, if like many people you've always been a road rider, it's worth giving the other types of cycling a try in case they suit you better. And even if you're never going to be Chris Hoy, make sure that at least once in your life, you experience riding the banked track of a velodrome. It will be the fastest you've ever ridden and the most fun you've ever had.

POCKET PACKING

Those capacious pockets on the back of a cycling jersey are there to stow everything you need for a day ride. Here's what you should pack:

- A mini pump, tyre levers and a spare inner tube
- Weather protection, be it arm warmers for cold starts, a wind shell or a rainproof
- Phone, cash and bank card
- Nutritious snacks
- Sun protection, including SPF lip salve, on sunny days
- Multitool

ride smarter

training

Riding performance depends on how effectively your heart can fuel your muscles, and how strong those muscles are. The best way to improve cardio fitness is by doing interval and endurance training on a bike, whether that bike is out on the road, in a gym or mounted on a turbo trainer at home (good in winter). Monitoring your heart rate and cadence allows for precision plans.

There's no need to train for the occasional weekend ride, but if you have an upcoming event you know will stretch you, want to get in shape over winter for more ambitious summer riding or would just like to get up hills more easily, start work about 10 weeks in advance. Your national cycling organisation should be able to suggest a programme or put you in touch with a local coach. Cycle magazines and websites are useful (training.bikeradar. com, for example, offers an interactive training programme and diary) and some ride organizers post plans online.

It's worth doing some strength work, too. You need to develop both the muscles used directly in cycling and those that support them. Exercises such as lunges and squats will help power up your legs, and sit-ups for your abs, gentle back raises and other core work such as Pilates, will help keep your posture strong, balanced and pain-free.

STAIRMASTER

If you don't have much time for training, just take the stairs. Running up a few flights is great exercise for the quadriceps and calves, and gets your heart going too.

nutrition

Your food is your fuel, so it's important to eat the right things at the right time. The evening before a ride have an early dinner that includes both protein and carbohydrates. In the morning, fuel up with a decent but not over-heavy breakfast of slow-burn (low GI) foods such as porridge. On the bike, you need to top up energy levels at least every couple of hours. Pre-empt an energy crash by snacking regularly. Proprietary energy bars and gels contain the right kind of carbohydrates in the right proportions, but dried fruit, flapjack and bananas are just as convenient and do much the same job. Keep your water bottles topped up and drink from them often. If you're working hard in a hot climate, use an electrolyte product to replace lost body salts.

After a demanding ride, take some protein on board. A low-fat milkshake or a handful of nuts will do the job.

Events to aim for:
a miscellany of the world's best rides

CRITICAL MASS
Where? Cities worldwide
How hard? 1/5
What? Critical Mass rides take place in hundreds of cities all around the world, from Aberdeen to Zurich, at around 5.30pm on the last Friday of every month. The rides are self-organizing, but their loose aim is for human-powered vehicles to temporarily reclaim the streets by dint of sheer volume and niceness. They're fun, social and also thought-provoking and political.

LONDON TO PARIS
Where? The clue's in the name
How hard? 3/5
What? London to Paris is a favourite cycle challenge and many charities run supported rides. It's a tough nearly 500-km (190-mile) run with more climbing than you might expect, but the exhilaration of the finish along the Champs d'Elysées is hard to beat.

WORLD NAKED BIKE RIDE

Where? Lots of places, mainly towns and cities in the West
How hard? 2/5 (one for the ride, one for the cheek/s)
What? An attention-grabbing street party to raise the visibility of cycling (it works!). Participants are asked to go as bare as they dare, but full nudity isn't required, and body art is all part of the fun. As you might expect, WNBR takes place in the balmy days of summer, which means the date varies with the location.

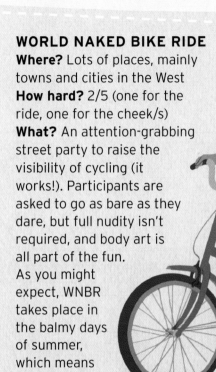

TWEED RIDES/RUNS

Where? Several cities in the UK, USA, Canada and Australia
How hard? 1/5
What? These moustache-twirling retro rides celebrate the tweedy spirit of cycling, with participants dressing up in period costume and mounting appropriate and even vintage steeds.

THE END TO END

Where? John O'Groats (Scotland) to Land's End (England)
How hard? 4/5
What? The 1450-1610-km (900-1,000-mile) ride from mainland UK's north-easternmost point to its far south-western extremity is a coveted achievement. Organizers offer tours of various durations to allow for different abilities. Much of the route is on the UK's Sustrans cycle route network, so it's possible to ride it independently.

TOUR LA NUIT

Where? Montréal, Canada
How hard? 1/5
What? A mass ride of 17,000 participants under the night sky, with lights a-winking and traffic-free streets: it's a once-in-a-lifetime experience and, at just 23 km (14 miles), is accessible to all. If you're visiting specially, you can even take part on one of the city's public bikes. The Tour is part of Montréal's cycling festival, which also includes a longer, traffic-free day ride.

MASS RIDE ETIQUETTE

- Don't make any sudden moves without looking behind you
- If you overtake someone, call out first
- As a courtesy, point out any hazards on the road and shout out to riders behind if a car is approaching
- Take care not to drop your water bottle as it may cause an accident
- If you are pulling to one side or rejoining the ride, wait for a safe gap in the 'traffic'

FIVE BORO BIKE TOUR

Where? New York, USA
How hard? 2/5
What? It's the world's biggest mass ride in one of its most awesome cities: over 30,000 participants ride 64 km (40 miles) around all five of New York's boroughs, crossing five bridges, taking one ferry and having the streets all to themselves for one blissful day. It's organized by non-profit cycle advocates Bike New York on the first Sunday of every May.

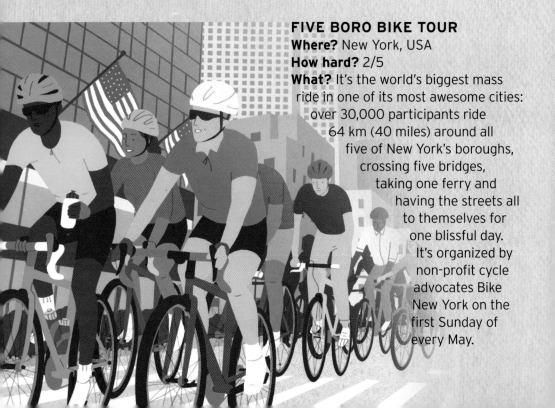

ETAPE DU TOUR
Where? France
How hard? 5/5
What? This is the mother of them all: a cyclosportive ridden on the route of an actual mountain stage of the Tour de France, just before the Tour itself comes to town. It's open to all (and many thousands take part), but it will take serious training to get up some vicious gradients, and you'll need a doctor's certificate!

RAGBRAI
Where? Across Iowa, USA
How hard? 3/5
What? This quirky, compelling ride takes 10,000 or so riders right across the state of Iowa, from the Missouri to the Mississippi – it's around 805 km (500 miles) in a week. You'll experience outstanding Midwestern hospitality all along the way, and great entertainment at the overnight tent stops (your gear is carried for you).

LAKE TAUPO CYCLE CHALLENGE
Where? New Zealand
How hard? 3/5
What? New Zealand's largest lake has a jaw-dropping setting in a volcanic crater. The Cycle Challenge includes a century ride all the way around it, along with mountain bike and tandem events and races for men, women and kids. It's held on the last Saturday of November.

LOVING AND GIVING
Lots of popular organized rides hold back places for cyclists prepared to raise money for a charity, and some charities stage events themselves. These vary from short one-day events that are a great way to get your first proper ride behind you – they're supported, and there's a great vibe – to big life-changing challenges, such as crossing Cuba, or going from the Andes to the Amazon. Riders pledging a big wodge of sponsor money pay little or nothing for the experience. It's a win–win situation.

The useful bit at the back

NATIONAL CYCLESPORT BODIES

Bike NZ
bikenz.org.nz
British Cycling
britishcycling.org.uk
Cycling Australia
cycling.org.au
Cycling Canada
cyclingcanada.ca
Cycling South Africa
cyclingsa.com
USA Cycling
usacycling.org

NATIONAL CYCLING ORGANISATIONS

Adventure Cycling Association (USA)
adventurecycling.org
Austcycle (Australia)
austcycle.com.au
Cycling Advocacy Network (New Zealand)
can.org.nz
CTC (UK)
ctc.org.uk
Pedal Power Association (South Africa)
pedalpower.org.za

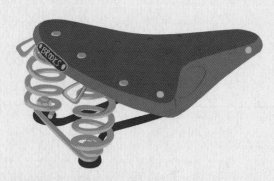

MEDIA

Bicyclefilmfestival.com
Travelling film and bike culture festival that's a load of fun.

bicycling.com
Big-hitting USA sport and leisure cycling magazine.

bikeradar.com
A stable of cycle mags covering all the disciplines, and a great free website.

cycling.tv
Pay-to-watch cyclesport streaming.

cyclingweekly.co.uk
The definitive road cyclesport magazine.

cyclosport.org
Good for event listings and more.

rouleurmagazine.cc
Gorgeous design and reverence for the road: style and substance.

sheldonbrown.com
Technical talk in depth.

http://thebikeshow.net
Ace UK-based radio show, available online.

urbanvelo.org
Great mag on city cycling, with free pdfs to download.

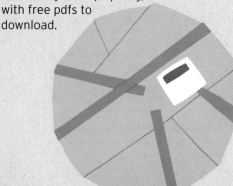

ONLINE RETAILERS

bobs-bicycles.com (USA)
chainreactioncycles.com (international)
decathlon.co.uk (UK)
jensonusa.com (USA)
wiggle.co.uk (international)

TOP TOUR OPERATORS

backroads.com
Mainly easy and comfortable, worldwide.

exodus.co.uk
Explorations worldwide.

headwater.com
Leisure and culture, mainly Europe.

sportingtours.co.uk
Europe: training camps, sportives, watch the classics.

trektravel.com
Easy explorations to seriously sporting.

BRILLIANT BLOGS

http://bicycledesign.net
bikesnobnyc.blogspot.com
crazyguyonabike.com
(portal to lots of bike travel blogs)
ecovelo.info
http://inrng.com
(cyclesport news and insight)

GLOSSARY

Aero-bar Handlebar extension allowing an aerodynamic tuck position

Air Something you get on a jump

ATB Another word for mountain bike

Audax Long-distance UK cycling event

Beading The textured edge of the tyre that sits inside the wheel rim

Beater A nothing-to-look-at bike for getting around town

Bidon Water bottle

Bonk An energy sag caused by lack of food

Bottom bracket Not a bracket, but the axle joining the chainset to the crank on the other side of the bike, through the frame

Cadence How fast you turn the pedals

Cassette A set of sprockets

Chainring A toothed gear ring attached to the pedal crank

Chainset One, two or three chainrings assembled together with the crank

Cleat The metal fitting on a cycle shoe that clips into the pedal

Clipless pedals Pedals that you can clip shoes into (confusingly)

Derailleur The tensioned gearing system that uses cables to move the chain onto different sprockets

Drafting Riding tight on the tail of another rider to benefit from their 'wind shadow'

Dropouts The notches that retain the wheels at the end of the forks fit

Forks The arms that extend down from the frame to hold the wheels

Granny gear Very low gear

Gripshift Motorbike-style gear shifter at end of handlebar

Hardtail A mountain bike without rear suspension

Headset The bearing that connects the front fork to the handlebar and allows it to turn within the frame

Hoods The casings around the brake levers on a road bike

Indexed Gears that click neatly into place

Jockey wheel The two tiny cogwheels in the rear mech

King of the Mountains The best climber in a road race

Keirin Track race that starts with riders following a special motorbike called a Derny

Lugs Connectors Connectors that link bike tubes into a frame

Musette Little bag for passing food to road cyclists

Omnium A sort of 'hextathlon' of track cycling, with six events

Peloton The main pack of riders in a road race

Rear mech The sticky-out derailleur mechanism that moves the chain between the sprockets on the back wheel

Salmoning Riding the wrong way up a one-way street

Singletrack A mountain bike trail wide enough for only one bike

Slickrock Exposed rock surface much beloved by mountain bikers

SPD Shimano Pedalling Dynamics – the most common clipless pedal and shoe system

Sprocket A cogged wheel attached to the hub of the rear wheel

Stem Links the handlebars to the frame

Trackstanding Standing on the pedals without turning them

Yellow Jersey The top worn by the leader of the Tour de France